Narrowboat on
The Trent

John Lower

The author's narrowboat *Madeley Wood* in Newark Town Lock

RICHLOW, ENGLAND
www.richlow.co.uk

Contents

Introduction..5
The Trent..7
Waterways only accessible from the Trent...............9
Cruising on the River Trent....................................11
Sound signals, Lights, VHF channels..................2,15
Large Mechanical Locks...16
The Non-tidal Trent..18
The Tidal Trent...23
Calculated cruising...23
When do I set off?..26
Tidal facilities..29
Entering locks from the tideway............................32
Contacts..37

Maps

Non-tidal river..18-19
Tidal river...30
Navigable Trent...Back cover

Copyright © John Lower, 2010

All rights reserved. No part of this publication may be reproduced or transmitted, in any form or by any means, without permission.

First published in 2007, and continuously updated by
Richlow - Sheffield S26, UK   books@richlow.co.uk
www.richlow.co.uk

Further updates are on www.richlowinfo.blogspot.co.uk

ISBN 978-0-9552609-3-3

A CIP catalogue record for this book is available from the British Library.

Introduction

This book is a personal record of how the crew of the narrowboat *Madeley Wood* go about cruising the River Trent. John and Barbara Lower have been navigating the tidal Trent for thirty years, first in a small cruiser and then in different narrowboats. In this book, they aim to share their experiences and thereby encourage other narrowboaters to use the Trent.

The Trent is 85 miles of mostly rural waterway to be explored. There are historic towns along its course, pleasant pubs, quiet out-of-the-way moorings and an abundance of wildlife. And, on the tidal section, a rare opportunity to see barges in action carrying sand, gravel or oil.

For those who have gained their boating experience on canals, the thought of cruising on a large river may be daunting, but narrowboats are much more stable and seaworthy than you would expect. They are a common sight on the Trent, both on the non-tidal and tidal sections. And it's not necessary to "do" the whole of the Trent in one go - get used to the "feel" of a river by cruising down to Cromwell Lock and, if you like the experience, try the tidal section another time. Remember - you can turn round anywhere, there's no need to find a winding hole!

Another difference is that the cosy reassurance of the towpath is lost, but if you think your boat is going to give problems - then do not cruise on a river.

Finally, the main difference is that the water moves - often faster than it does on the upper reaches of the Llangollen Canal! So always turn into the flow when you want to manoeuvre so that you have control of your boat. Remember that a river is a natural waterway - take note of the weather. If heavy rainfall has soaked the midlands recently then the flow on the Trent will be much faster, so perhaps delaying your cruise may be sensible. Tight cruising schedules and rivers do not mix.

And of course - when planning your cruise, you can always drive out to the locations and have a look so you know what to expect.

This book details our experiences of navigating the Trent, but it is not a guide book - it is intended to be used in conjunction with the excellent Trent Charts published by The Boating Association (formerly Trent Boating Association) and known locally as "Sissons Charts", which are highly recommended by the author. (page 37).

The Trent is an opportunity to test boating skills, and the chance to reach the delights of other non-crowded waterways - the Giant's Staircase of the Chesterfield Canal, a lovely rural waterway where there are no queues for locks, and where you can operate four sets of staircases in a beautiful setting without supervision. Or visit the Fossdyke and cruise through the Glory Hole in Lincoln - the only medieval bridge in Britain with buildings built on it.

So, give it a go. All I can do in this book is tell of our experiences gained over thirty years, but the final decision is yours - only you know the capabilities of your boat and its crew. Navigating the Trent should be seen as an exciting challenge requiring proper preparation and planning.

Respect the river, don't fear it.

The author's narrowboat Madeley Wood passing through the unique Glory Hole in Lincoln

6

The Trent

The Trent is England's third longest river, flowing 170 miles from north Staffordshire to the Humber estuary. Above Shardlow in Derbyshire the river is no longer used for navigation. Instead, boats use the adjacent Trent & Mersey Canal to reach the famous towns further upstream such as Burton-on-Trent and Stoke-on-Trent.

This book includes the navigable section of the Trent commonly used by narrowboats - that is downstream from Shardlow at the end of the Trent & Mersey Canal, as far as Keadby, the junction with the Sheffield & South Yorkshire navigations. Within those miles, the Trent is a river of great variety, almost straining belief that it is one waterway. From the popular marina and locks at Sawley, one travels through the busy urban conurbation that is Nottingham, passing a famous Sheriff's castle, then past rowing-club-lined banks and the National Watersports Centre. Picturesque villages and countryside mark the river down to the historic market town of Newark. Further on Cromwell Weir marks the start of the tidal river which has higher flood banks, prudent flood-meadows, dominant power stations and the shipping wharves at Keadby.

Little that we see today is natural river - the Trent is too important for that. Throughout recorded history it has been a trading artery with man striving to improve its navigable qualities - to take his larger and larger boats further upstream. The modern Trent is based on the major engineering schemes carried out in the 1790s. Greater water depth is achieved by the level being held up by weirs spaced throughout the 38 miles from Sawley to Cromwell, with locks for boats to navigate the change of level.

But no matter how beneficial the Trent's use for water transport may be, navigational improvements must never interfere with the river's most important function - the drainage of a vast area of England. Six million people rely on the Trent and its many tributaries for the natural drainage of the 6,500 square miles in which they live. Therefore, where the construction of a lock would narrow the river too much, an artificial channel is made called a 'cut'.

The lock and other navigational paraphernalia is built in the channel - as in Sawley Cut and Cranfleet Cut - and the river is left free to bypass it by flowing unhindered along its own course.

Cromwell, as the furthest downstream weir and largest lock, is where the Trent undergoes its greatest transformation. Above the weir it is a man-controlled deep river, as it has been since leaving Sawley - lined by towns and villages. Below Cromwell Weir the Trent is open to the sea, its last fifty miles subject to natural tidal forces. As a result, the river immediately becomes more remote, most buildings keeping their distance behind flood defences - meadows, walls and banks.

The Trent is a coarse fishery. When we started cruising it, the banks would be lined with fishermen at weekends, sometimes the channel would be marked by men in waders. Nowadays we seem to see less piscators, whether the hobby or the river is less popular I know not. More recently, salmon have been returning to the river and improvements are being made to help them climb the weirs.

It is also a commercial waterway. Coasters, which formerly made their way as far upstream as Gainsborough, now only reach Keadby where the lifting bridge is fixed across the river. Large barges operate throughout the tidal length carrying sand and gravel and occasionally oil. They are rarely seen above Cromwell Lock on the non-tidal river.

Certain lengths of the river (both tidal and non-tidal) are used by water skiers, keep a look out for signs marking the "water ski zones".

Dinghy-sailing, rowing and canoeing take place on the river. Take particular care between Sawley Lock and Trent Lock, and from Meadow Lane Lock to Holme Lock. And the National Watersports Centre adjacent to Holme Lock also spawns large inflatable rafts.

If all this seems daunting, bear in mind that there are many narrowboats on the Trent every day.

Water skiing at Gunthorpe

Waterways Only Accessible from the Trent

The Trent is approached from the south and midlands via the Trent & Mersey Canal or the River Soar. From the Yorkshire waterways, the approach is via the Stainforth & Keadby Canal, part of the Sheffield & South Yorkshire navigations.

From the Non-tidal Section

Erewash Canal
Part of the Grand Union system, fifteen broad locks lift this twelve-mile waterway from Trent Lock to Langley Mill through a mainly urban landscape along the Derbyshire-Nottinghamshire border. Ambitious restoration plans would further extend this navigation along the Cromford Canal and deep into the Peak District.

Grantham Canal
Currently un-navigable, but is the subject of a lengthy restoration campaign. The original waterway left the Trent next to the Nottingham Forest football ground and meandered across thirty-three miles of rural Nottinghamshire and Leicestershire. A restored waterway is likely to have a new junction near the National Watersports Centre below Holme Lock.

From the Tidal Section

The Fossdyke & the Witham Navigations
Running forty-three miles from Torksey across the flat Lincolnshire countryside, these broad waterways are considered to be the oldest in the country - it is claimed that the Fossdyke was built and navigated by the Romans. Some of the route lies between high floodbanks, but there is much of interest along these waterways. In addition to the well known attractions of historic Lincoln and Boston, boaters can visit a number of windmills, steam pumping-stations, castles and the RAF Battle of Britain Memorial Flight. It is also possible to

cruise the quaintly named Witham Navigable Drains, whilst current restoration plans will extend navigation on the Slea navigations and open up the Horncastle Canal. For the future there are ambitious plans to link Boston with the River Nene at Peterborough creating a new Lincolnshire Cruising Ring. The first phase of which, the Black Sluice Navigation, opened in 2009. (Richlow publish a Lincolnshire Waterways guide, - see page 39).

Chesterfield Canal

Built to the design of the famous 18th century engineer James Brindley, this attractive narrow canal runs 46 miles from West Stockwith to its name town with its famous twisted spire. Presently 31 miles are navigable from the Trent, passing through pretty countryside and the towns of Retford and Worksop. The energetic Chesterfield Canal Trust is spearheading the restoration of the remainder. Of particular interest is the beautiful "Giants Staircase" of locks carrying the waterway to its summit level - the flight contains a unique mixture of two-rise and three-rise staircases mixed in with the normal single chambers. (Richlow publish a Chesterfield Canal guide - see page 39).

River Idle

An historic commercial route which was superseded in the eighteenth century by the building of the Chesterfield Canal. The Idle is a quiet, remote and rural waterway which runs eleven miles between flood banks from West Stockwith to Bawtry. It is rarely navigated since the Environment Agency introduced a very large fee to open the sluices at the entrance to admit boats. Local bodies such as the Retford & Worksop Boat Club periodically organise group cruises on the river.

A Retford & Worksop Boat Club cruise emerges from the River Idle at West Stockwith

Cruising on the River Trent

Before setting out

Check your boat **insurance** covers you for the tidal Trent. Most Inland Waterway Policies include a statement similar to: *"Cruising Range – Inland non-tidal waters of the United Kingdom (tidal access to the inland system is included)"*. I have checked with our insurers who confirmed that we can cruise as far downstream as Keadby but not further towards the Humber or round Trent Falls unless we are in a convoy. All insurance policies are different so for peace of mind, it is worth a phone call or letter to check cover and see if any special conditions apply.

As part of the Canal & River Trust campaign against **licence** evasion, its lock-keepers on the Trent will refuse passage to any boat not displaying a current licence. (Although Associated British Ports is the navigation authority for the tidal Trent from Gainsborough Bridge to the Humber, no additional licence is required).

Check lock opening hours, and for stoppages. This is particularly important for "winter hours" where opening times are much reduced and notice may need to be given. And despite global warming, "winter" according to the CRT seems to get longer each year - "winter" 2006 was from the end of September until Easter!

Boat and Equipment

When we plan to cruise on the Trent, or indeed any river, we ensure that our boat is in good condition. Firstly that the engine is running properly, that we have plenty of fuel, that the lubricant and coolant levels are OK and we have carried out all our routine checks.

Life-jackets or buoyancy aids must be available for all the crew. We wear ours in locks and on the tidal section, or when the river is running fast.

Longer mooring **ropes** are needed, especially at West Stockwith and Keadby locks, where the ropes are usually passed round a lock-side bollard and then the further end handed back to the boat crew. About 40ft ropes are recommended, though on *Madeley Wood* we carry 50ft "go-anywhere" ropes as this is the length required by the Manchester Ship Canal Company.

Beg, borrow or buy an **anchor** that is big enough to hold your boat on the river. *Madeley Wood* (42ft) has a 15kg Danforth anchor which has been tested and holds on the current. This should be satisfactory for most narrowboats.

To be effective, the length of the anchor **cable** must be at least three times the depth of the water. On *Madeley Wood*, we have 30ft of chain attached directly to the anchor to ensure it drags flat on the river bed. Attached to that is at least 50ft of strong rope.

It may be common sense but I will say it anyway - the anchor cable must be **attached** to the boat! And the part of the boat it is attached to must be strong enough to take the sudden shock when the anchor bites in the river bed. Also, it is no good the anchor being below decks in case it is needed – it should be set up on deck ready to deploy whenever you are on any river (even when moored on the non tidal sections). On *Madeley Wood*, we tie the extreme end of the cable to an anchor point installed by the boat builder under the gunnels. If we deploy the anchor, we try to let it down gently and then gradually take the strain on the "T" stud. But if that stud were to fail or the rope slipped through our hands, then it is still attached. Finally, the anchor must be easily accessible by the crew without the need to walk along the gunnels.

We find a pair of **binoculars** very helpful for checking activity at locks and reading signs well in advance. (They are also handy for spotting wildlife: we like bird-watching and have seen seals on a couple of occasions.)

"*River Trent (Tidal), Cromwell Lock to Trent Falls - Version 10*", published by The Boating Association (formerly Trent Boating Association). Although the river looks big and wide and is navigated by huge barges, there are shallows, sandbanks and other obstructions which can catch out the unwary narrowboater, especially at low tide and when there is not much fresh water in the river after dry weather. In our early boating years we once ran *Madeley*

Wood, through inattention to the charts.

For many years the TBA has published Trent **charts** as easy to follow, clear line-drawings, and I have always recommended them as a "must have". However, their latest update (version 10 published in 2011) is an entirely new format based on aerial photography and, in my view, the pages are cluttered and difficult to follow, and therefore look very off-putting. On balance, I would say boaters do need a copy, but better still, try to obtain a copy of an old edition. See p37 for where to purchase the current version).

Night time cruising is not recommended, however navigation lights are required when cruising at dawn or dusk or in poor visibility. (Page 15).

VHF radio is useful (see p15). All the locks and commercial craft have it and also many of the private boats, but it is not compulsory and a mobile phone can generally be used to ring a lock-keeper. **If you will be reliant on a mobile phone for communications it is important to have an on-board facility to**

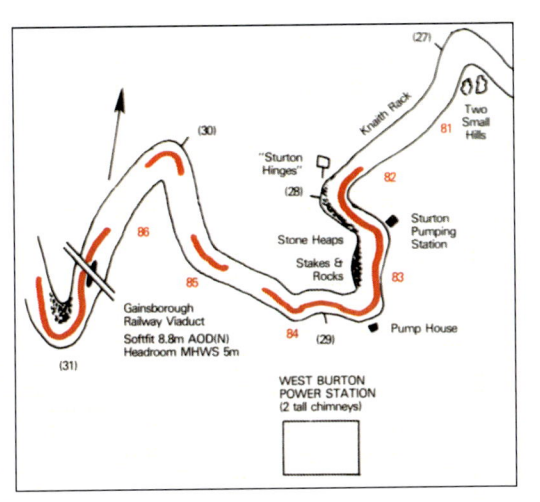

Above - extract from a typical page of the **old** version of The Boating Association Charts showing in red how the channel is marked. CRT has installed Kilometre Posts along their section which can easily be referenced to the chart.

Below - extract from the **new** version.

recharge it. (To use VHF, it is necessary to have an Operator's Licence and your boat must also be registered. Page 38).

Setting Off

Before venturing onto the tidal Trent, I always arrange to **arrive** at the entrance lock at least an hour before my predicted tide time, as this gives me the opportunity to contact the lock keeper, check the engine, anchor and lifejackets, and pass through the lock.
Chatting to the lock-keeper, I ensure that the lock-keeper at my destination has been notified to expect me. Lock-keepers are often founts of useful local knowledge and may know of, for example, large commercial craft in action on the river or dredging operations in progress. They will also know the whereabouts of other pleasure craft on the river - their presence is reassuring if you do run into any difficulties. (Hint - take your charts when you go to see the keepers so you know where they are talking about.).

Look at the **weather forecast**. I never venture out onto the tidal river if the wind forecast is 25 mph or more. Wind over tide (that is, the wind blowing in the opposite direction to that in which the tide is flowing) can create some quite large waves, especially on the long straight reaches below Gainsborough. High water levels after heavy rainfall can also close the Navigation, especially above Nottingham, or cause slow-going against the fresh water coming down the river.

When cruising **concentrate** on the river. Keep a sharp eye open for commercial craft and be prepared to pass them on the "wrong side" on sharp bends or near shallows. Remember they need the deep water. Also keep a good look out behind - barges and large cruisers catch you up very quickly.

Dredging often takes place on the river. The dredger displays a pair of metal "flags" or boards on its cabin top - one red, one white. Carefully pass the work on the side displaying the white flag (there are often cables and ropes reaching to the bank on the red flag side).

We always keep the **front cabin doors** of *Madeley Wood* firmly closed to ensure no waves, spray or wash from passing craft can enter the cabin.

Know your sound signals and check your **horn** is working. If it is a feeble car-horn type, buy or borrow something louder, perhaps a portable airhorn operated by an aerosol can.

Sound Signals
It is important to know these signals, both to sound them and to recognise the intentions of other craft. They are listed inside the front cover, for speedy access on the river.

Lights
Lights as follows must be shown when navigating between sunset and sunrise or in restricted visibility.
A bright WHITE light on the mast or staff at the bow, not less than 1.2 metres (4 feet) above the hull.
A GREEN light on the starboard (right) side.
A RED light on the port (left) side.
A WHITE light on the stern.

VHF Working Frequencies
Canal & River Trust Locks - channel 74

Official frequencies for Associated British Ports, for the Trent from Gainsborough Bridge to the Humber. Calling & Listening - channel 15
Intership - channel 10

Barges - from experience, I have found that barges monitor and communicate on channel 6 (intership) above Gainsborough Bridge, and often use this channel down to Keadby too.

CRT has put warning notices at the worst shallows. They are difficult to read from a distance without binoculars. (I once boated across the river to read one - only to find it said "Danger Keep Away"!)

Large Mechanical Locks

Below Nottingham - Down to the Tideway

All the locks below Nottingham, down to the tidal Trent, may be operated by lock-keepers during the summer but can be operated by boaters when the keeper is not on duty. (Map pages 18-19).

All the locks have decent landings above and below.

Traffic lights are installed at the locks:

•   If a green light is displayed, the lock is ready for you to enter.

•   If a red light is displayed, the lock is set against you. Try a long blast on the horn or call the lock-keeper on VHF Marine Band radio, channel 74. If the red continues to be shown, then it's time to tie up and walk to find the lock-keeper.

•   If a red and a green light are displayed, the lock is set against you but the lock-keeper is aware you are there and is turning the lock round for you. (Do not enter the lock as soon as the gates open but wait for the green light - there might be another boat waiting to emerge).

•   If an orange light is displayed over the traffic lights, then the lock-keeper is off duty and you must work the lock yourself. Tie up and familiarise yourself with the lock controls before starting the operation.

Each set of gates and paddles is operated by a separate console mounted on the lockside. Insert the CRT Watermate (Sanitary Station) key into the console and follow the instructions to fill or empty the lock and then open the gates. The key cannot be removed until the gates and all the paddle are closed.

When the boat has entered the lock, you will find wires mounted in vertical recesses at intervals along the lock walls. Bow and stern ropes should be passed round the wires and returned to the boat to control it as the water level changes. (It is easier to use the wires rather than the lock side bollards unless you are single-handing).

When ascending, we always stay as near the back of the chamber as we can (allowing for other boats sharing the lock with us). The water is more turbulent near the top gates and thus a boat there is harder to control.

Once the boat is under control and the gates closed, move to the console at the other end of the lock and repeat the process.

On leaving the lock, you will have to close the gates to get your key back. (If another boat is coming the other way, do not be surprised if their lock operator offers to swap keys with you, thus avoiding the need to close the gates and reopen them again).

Notes:

When on duty, the lock-keepers monitor VHF channel 74 and keep in contact with each other both by radio and telephone, so once you have passed through one lock, they will notify the next that you are coming. If you are planning to stop, it is courteous to let them know your intentions.

All the locks on the river have sanitary stations and taps but sometimes they are a distance from the visitor moorings.

Barbara operates the control console to open the bottom gates of Stoke Bardolph Lock

17

The Non-tidal Trent

On the canals, it is usually possible to moor up along the towpath anywhere we feel like. But this is not true for rivers. In most places the banks are private property, there can be shallows near the banks and water levels vary. Mostly we find it a good idea to stop only at recognised, designated moorings.

I have listed the moorings and facilities we like to use on the non-tidal Trent. As the majority of boaters visiting for the first time are from the midlands canals, I have listed them from Derwent Mouth Lock on the Trent & Mersey Canal. Distances given are from Derwent Mouth Lock.

Derwent Mouth
It is possible to cruise up the River Trent (turn right below the lock) for a mile or so past Shardlow Marina and Cavendish Bridge. There are no public moorings along this section.

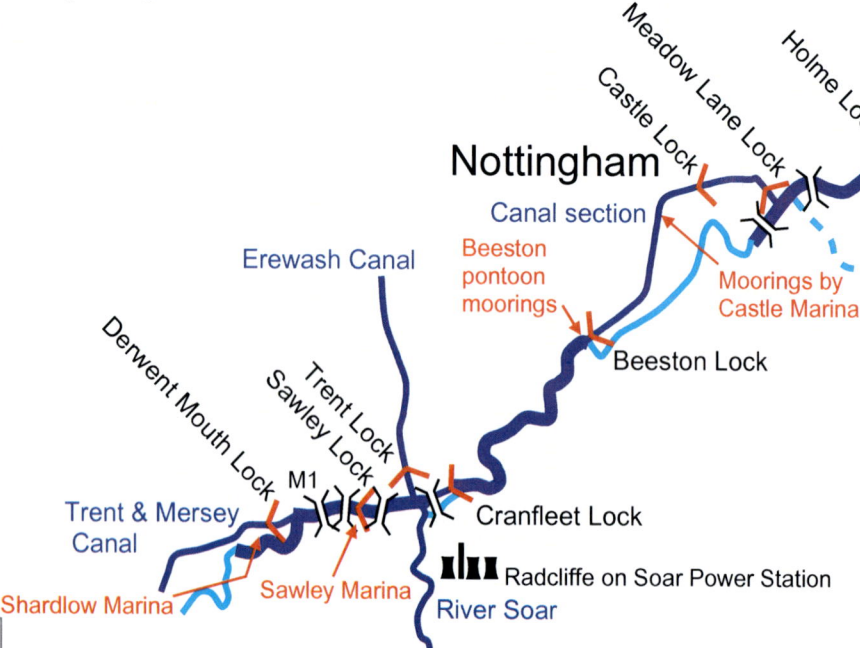

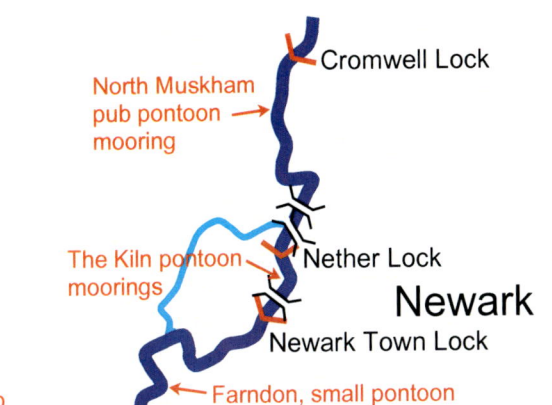

Cromwell Lock
North Muskham pub pontoon mooring
The Kiln pontoon moorings
Nether Lock
Newark
Newark Town Lock
Fiskerton, small pub pontoon
Farndon, small pontoon
Hazelford Lock
Gunthorpe pontoon moorings
Gunthorpe Lock
Stoke Bardolph Lock

Grantham Canal

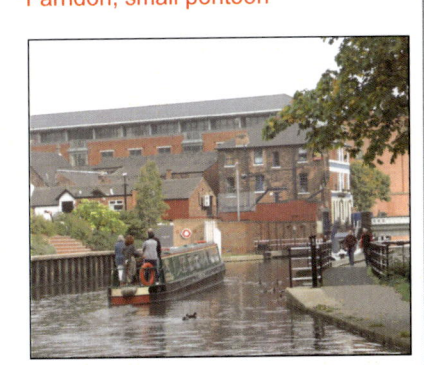

Approaching Castle Lock, Nottingham

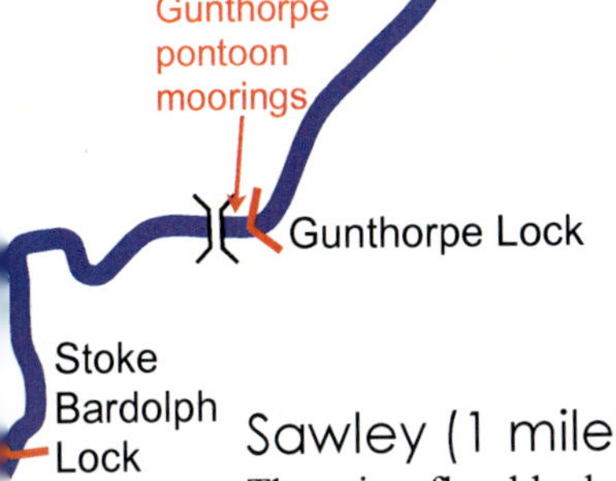

Sawley (1 mile)

There is a flood lock which is usually left open, but is operated like a normal canal lock when river levels are higher.

Moorings opposite the Marina give access to two pubs - the Plank & Leggit along the road and the Harrington Arms over the river bridge. A very useful chandlery and all services are at Sawley Marina. Visitor moorings at the Marina are free during the day but there is an overnight charge.

There are two parallel locks available for use and often operated by a lock-keeper. Traffic lights (see page 16) indicate if they are on duty. The sanitary station is more easily accessed from a pontoon on the river channel below the locks

Trent Lock and Cranfleet Cut (2 miles)

Junction with the River Soar and the Erewash Canals.

19

Good visitor moorings in the start of Cranfleet Cut give access to the two pubs. On the river, there is also a floating pontoon mooring for patrons of the Navigation Inn. Floodgates by the railway bridge may be shut with high river levels, preventing navigation. Sometimes they will appear shut but are not locked. Go through but leave them as found.

Cranfleet to Beeston
Look out for warning arrows marking the way to avoid shallows. Approaching Beeston Lock there are limited visitor moorings on the floating pontoon and a boatyard with chandlery, fuel etc, a café and pub.

Meadow Lane Lock

Beeston Cut, Nottingham and the Nottingham Canal (10-13 miles)
The lock leads into a three-mile canal section through Nottingham. There are sanitary stations both here and where the canal rejoins the river at Meadow Lane Lock. Whilst it is possible to moor anywhere along the canal, we choose to tie-up north (downstream) of Castle Marina which is convenient for a number of pubs and restaurants and also for shopping at Sainsburys. Castle Marina has all the usual boaters needs. It is a reasonable walk from here to the city centre. Below Castle Lock the old canal warehouses have been converted into bars and we find this is **NOT** a good place to spend the night!

Holme Lock (15 miles)
There are good moorings above the lock where we like to moor to watch the canoeists and white-water rafters using the National Watersports centre alongside. This is the first of the huge mechanised locks (see page16). There is a rubbish skip near the lock, and a sanitary station on the lock side.

Stoke Bardolph Lock (18 miles)
Pleasant, quiet visitor moorings above the lock.

Ferry Boat Inn (19miles)
About a mile below Stoke Bardolph Lock. We like to moor here but the mooring is very basic and can be shallow, so take great care. Lots of swans and wildfowl here - watch where you put your feet! Mooring is much easier at Gunthorpe.

Gunthorpe (23 miles)
We think Gunthorpe is the best overnight mooring on the river, a pleasant village with a choice of pubs and a restaurant. There are visitor moorings on a floating pontoon near the bridge and if these get full on summer weekends, additional moorings in the entrance to the lock-cut above the lock. There is a café, and a deluxe sanitary station with palatial showers.

Hazelford Lock (28 miles)
Visitor mooring above and below the lock This is a quiet out-of-the-way place ideal for a BBQ. At the moorings above the lock the river wall is high necessitating climbing the ladders or clambering across the roof of the boat.

Fiskerton (30 miles)
Floating pontoon mooring for patrons of the Bromley Arms but it is only about 70ft long. It is unusual to find a mooring space here but if you can, the pub makes a stop well worthwhile and there is a nearby village shop.

Farndon (33 miles)
Another floating pontoon, with very limited moorings (half of it is dedicated to a tripboat). Pub and village. There are visitor moorings at the nearby Farndon Harbour (marina) but I have to confess we have never visited them.

Newark (36 miles)
An historic town which we like exploring. The best moorings are on a floating pontoon below the lock and ancient river bridge (Waitrose supermarket behind the CRT offices). The moorings opposite the castle are nearer to town but high above the water involving a scramble over the boat roof. There are chandleries at both the marinas.

Newark Nether Lock (37 miles)
There are visitor moorings below the lock but we have not over-nighted here because of the close proximity of the railway.

North Muskham (40 miles).
One of our favourite moorings, floating finger pontoons for patrons of the excellent Muskham Ferry pub. Do take care when approaching the moorings - the river current across the moorings can sweep you sidewards into other moored boats.

Cromwell Lock (42 miles)
Gateway to the tidal river. Pleasant and quiet visitor moorings above the lock. Great if you have to catch an early tide the next day and want to consult with the lock-keeper beforehand.

Tidal Trent

Calculated Cruising

Tides occur roughly every thirteen hours. ***Flood*** is when the tide starts travelling inland against the natural current of the river. On the Trent it changes direction very quickly. ***Flood Tide*** is when the tide is running in. It lasts approximately 2½ hours and the flow is very fast until the water levels increase to ***High Water***. The tide then turns and the falling tide is known as the ***Ebb*** and lasts approximately 10 hours. Most narrowboats can make little headway against the tide and thus I try to plan my journey to travel with the tide, with consequently shorter journey times, less stress on the engine, and fuel saved.

When planning my journey on the tidal Trent, I first purchase a set of **Tide Tables** (see page 38). Lock keepers will also provide the information, but I find a great deal of satisfaction from working out my own journey times. Indeed for boaters resident on the Chesterfield Canal, as we often are, the ability to work out tide times for different weekends often governs the choice of the holiday week, with the intention of avoiding having to get up too early in the morning to catch the tide!

It may seem strange, but the first chart in the tide tables is "**Phases of the Moon**". This is because tides are caused by the gravitational pull of the moon on the world's great oceans. But how does this affect the Trent? It means that as the position of the moon can be worked out in advance, so can the tides. And the size of the tides varies with the phase of the moon. The larger and faster-running tides are called ***Spring Tides*** and occur two or three days after full or new moons. The smaller, slower-flowing tides are called ***Neap Tides,*** and occur at half moons.

The rest of the tide tables booklet is devoted to tide times and heights. Depending on the version you buy, they give tides at a variety of locations. For the purposes of examples in this chapter, I will use the times given at Hull Albert Dock which seems to appear in all the different versions.

Date	Day	Time of high water, Albert Dock (Morning)	Depth of water, Albert Dock (H m)	Time of high water, Albert Dock (Afternoon)	Depth of water, Albert Dock (H m)
1	Sa	09:25	7.8	22:05	7.3

Extract from tide table for July 1st 2006 - high water

Important. *Times are usually given as GMT (Greenwich Mean Time) and so an hour has to be added during British Summer Time (BST)*. This is the time of year when most first-time Trent visitors will be on the tideway.

Note. *High Tide* does not occur at the same time all along the river, but travels upriver from the Humber like a wave. The following table is an estimation of the *Flow* duration (the time the water flows inland and the water levels increase) and the difference in *High Water* times at each of the river junctions relative to Hull Albert Dock.

Junction / Lock	Flow duration	High Water
Keadby	2hr 45min	+1hr 15min
West Stockwith	2hr 30min	+2hr
Torksey	2hr	+3hr 45min
Cromwell	1hr	+4hr 15min

So *High Water* at any of the entry points onto the river can be predicted.
Example for West Stockwith on July 1st 2006 - *High Water* at Hull Albert Dock was 09:25 (from tide tables). Add 01:00 (one hour for British Summer Time) plus 02:00 (two hours from above table - *High Water* at West Stockwith) = 12:25. (Another tide occurred after midnight but this is of little interest to the pleasure boater!) **It must be borne in mind that prediction of tide times is not an exact science** and times can be affected by storms and wind directions in the North Sea and the amount of water (fresh) running over Cromwell Weir from inland areas.

Next, check the lock opening hours. This can vary from year to year, so it is advisable to check with the relevant lock-keepers before finalising your plans. It is best to book at least 24 hours in advance. We usually enquire well ahead and set a date - if this has to be moved forward or backward as we are not running on our planned schedule, then re-arranging is usually easily accommodated.

The following table shows the distance between the locks and typical times taken to complete each stage by our two differing narrowboats.

	Distance	Madeley Wood 2 (27HP)	Madeley Wood 1 (13HP)
Keadby ↕ West Stockwith	13 miles	1hr 30min	2hr 30min
↕ Torksey	14 miles	1hr 45min	2hr 30min
↕ Cromwell	16 miles	2hr 45min	3hr 30min

I usually draw a rough graph to work out first and last departure and arrival times. Below is an example. Calculation of optimum time (BST) to set out from West Stockwith to Torksey with *High Water* at Hull at 09:25 (GMT).

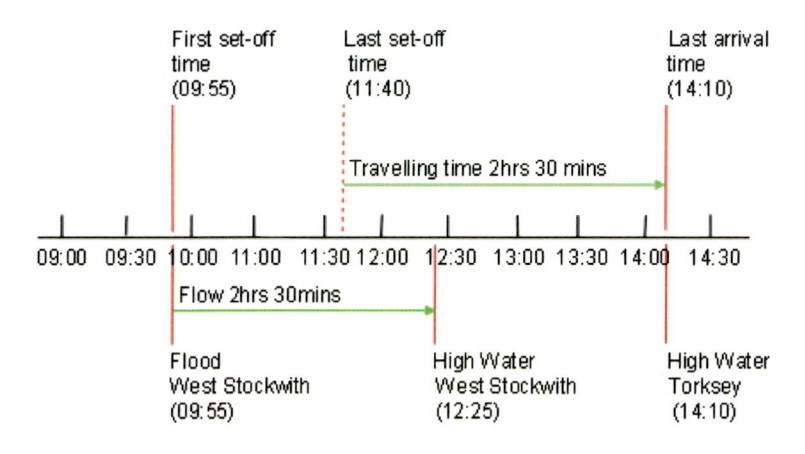

In this example, the last time I would wish to arrive at Torksey is *High Water* (14:10). The earliest time to leave West Stockwith is about 09:55. On our old, slow-moving narrowboat, journey time would be 2½ hours, so my last departure time would be 11:40. I usually like to allow a little extra time, or go as soon as possible, to cater for any unexpected delay.

25

When Do I Set Off?

As all the tidal locks are operated by lock-keepers, generally you have to go when they tell you. However, knowing which state of the tide to set off helps in planning the trip.

It is advisable to discuss and book your journey at least 24 hours ahead during summer working hours. During winter working hours, more notice is required.

Ensure that the lock-keeper at your destination knows you are coming. If you change your plans for any reason, let the lock-keepers know!

Going Downstream

From Cromwell to Torksey
Travel on the *Ebb* to reach Torksey before *Flood* - it will then be necessary to tie up on the pontoons to wait for sufficient water over the cill to enter the lock. **Diesel** can be bought above the lock, but telephone ahead to check availability, see page 38.

From Cromwell to West Stockwith
There are two ways of cruising down to Stockwith, dependant on tide and river conditions. The lock-keeper will advise which is the best for the day you are travelling.

(1)   Cruise down on the *Ebb* to reach Torksey before *Flood* and tie up on the pontoons outside Torksey Lock. Let the worst of the *Flood* pass the end of the cut and set off one hour before *High Water*. Now push the tide, it will turn before Gainsborough and carry you down to West Stockwith.

(2)   Cruise all the way to Gainsborough on the *Ebb* and tie up here before *Flood*. Set off again when the speed of the incoming tide has reduced, half an hour before *High Water* is due at West Stockwith. You will reach Stockwith Lock near *High Water Slack* making it easier to enter. THIS SECOND OPTION MUST NOT BE USED ON LARGE SPRING TIDES WHEN THERE IS AN AEGRE FORECAST. (Pages 28 and 38).

From Cromwell to Keadby

There are two ways of cruising down to Keadby, dependant on tide and river conditions. The lock keeper will advise which is the best for the day you are travelling

(1)   Cruise down on the *Ebb* to reach Torksey before flood and tie up on the pontoons outside Torksey Lock. Let the worst of the *Flood* pass the end of the cut and set off one hour before *High Water*. Now push the tide, it will turn before Gainsborough and carry you down to Keadby.

(2)   Cruise to Gainsborough on the *Ebb* and tie up here before *Flood*. Set off again when the speed of the incoming tide has reduced, half an hour before *High Water* is due at West Stockwith. THIS SECOND OPTION MUST NOT BE USED ON LARGE SPRING TIDES WHEN THERE IS AN AEGRE FORECAST. (Pages 28 and 38).

Going Upstream

From Keadby to West Stockwith
Leave Keadby about one-hour after *Flood*. The aim is to get to West Stockwith at *High Water Slack*, making it easy to enter the lock.

From Keadby to Torksey
Leave Keadby at *Flood*. You will reach Torksey just before *High Water*.

From Keadby to Cromwell
Leave Keadby at *Flood*. The tide will have turned before you reach Cromwell but there should be no difficulty in pushing the current in the upper tidal reaches. Consider breaking your journey at Torksey and catching the tide the following day, especially if you have made slow progress as far as Torksey.

From West Stockwith to Torksey
Leave Stockwith at *Flood*. You will reach Torksey before *High Water*.

From West Stockwith to Cromwell
Leave Stockwith at *Flood*. The tide will turn before you reach Cromwell but there will be no difficulty in pushing the current in the upper reaches.

From Torksey to Cromwell

If you are on the pontoons outside the lock, the best time to leave is at *Flood*. If you are on the Fossdyke above the lock it is only possible to lock out from the Fossdyke for a short while around *High Water*. As the lock is operated by a lock-keeper, they will advise you of a departure time. Lock out as soon as there is sufficient water over the cill and set off. (The depth of water over the cill is dependant on the height of the tide and the amount of fresh water flowing in the river).

Aegre (or aegir)

Aegre is pronounced a-ger. On the Trent the leading edge of the tide coming in (the *Flood*) can occasionally be a tidal bore of a few inches to 5 feet high, flowing up to Torksey or beyond. Generally an aegre only forms when there is a tide with a height of over 8.5 metres at Hull, no fresh flood water coming down the Trent, and no wind. All this sounds very unsettling, - however if you plan your passage, as you should do, there is no need to be underway on the Trent at *Flood,* and there is an aegre timetable published by the Environment Agency to help you. (See page 38). But if you cannot avoid the aegre, meet it head-on in the middle of the river.

In Distress

Good planning means being ready for an emergency, perhaps involving others, and in this section "distress" means human life is threatened in anyway.

On VHF, call HM Coastguard (ch16) or VTS HUMBER (ch16 or ch12). On a mobile phone, call 999 and ask for HM Coastguard. Other incidents, groundings, collisions, etc should be reported to HM Coastguard **without** using the word "distress".

Channel markers for when the river is in flood. Red cylinders mark the left-hand (port) side heading inland from the sea, and green cones mark the starboard side

Tidal Facilities

There are only a few places to moor on the tidal Trent so it is generally regarded as a through transit route. It is inadvisable to moor to the river bank owing to the changes in river level with the tide. Distances given are from Derwent Mouth Lock.

Cromwell Lock (42 miles)
Pleasant and quiet visitor moorings above the lock together with water point, rubbish disposal and sanitary station

Dunham Bridge (53 miles)
Floating pontoon mooring. Over the bridge there are a couple of pubs half-a-mile walk away in the village of Dunham and there is also a pub in Newton on the road towards Lincoln

Torksey Lock (57 miles)

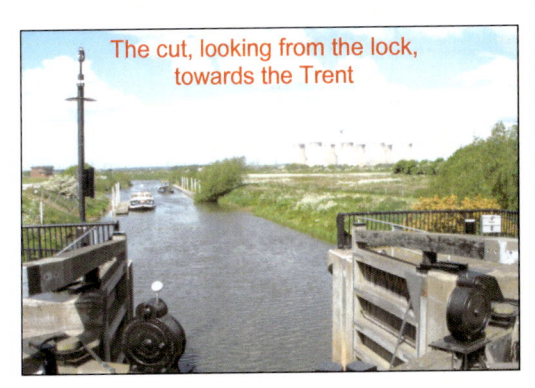

The cut, looking from the lock, towards the Trent

Floating pontoon moorings in the lock cut. Above the lock, all the usual boaters facilities including pump-outs, showers, diesel. Calor Gas from nearby Torksey Caravans. Basic food provisions are sold at the White Swan pub, which also serves excellent meals. There is a tea-room near the lock, with home-made cakes.

Stainforth & Keadby Canal (SSYN)
Keadby Bridge
Keadby Lock
M180 motorway
Sluice
Gainsborough
River Idle
West Stockwith Lock
Gainsborough Bridge
Mooring Pontoon
Railway Bridge
West Burton
Power Station
Chesterfield
Canal
Torksey Viaduct
Mooring Pontoons
Cottam Power
Station
Fossdyke &
Witham
Navigation
Torksey
Lock
Dunham Bridge
Mooring Pontoon
Fledborough Viaduct
Cromwell Lock

Madeley Wood at Gainsborough

Gainsborough (67 miles)
Floating pontoon moorings on the river - the gate at the top of the ramp is opened by a CRT "Watermate" sanitary station key. The moorings are operated by the local authority and there is a £2 charge - a ticket machine is located near the gate but has never worked when the author has visited. Good access for town shopping and to visit Gainsborough Old Hall.

West Stockwith (72 miles)
There are no visitor moorings on the river, so it is necessary to lock into the Chesterfield Canal for all the usual boaters facilities including pump-out, diesel, and a shower block. There are two pubs in the village.

Keadby (85 miles)
There are no visitor moorings on the river, so it is necessary to lock into the Stainforth & Keadby Canal for all the usual boaters facilities including a shower block.

Entering Locks from the Tideway

All the tidal locks are always operated by a lock-keeper - you cannot operate these locks yourself.

The lock-keepers monitor marine band radio, channel 74 and can also be contacted by telephone if you have a mobile.

Cromwell Lock
01636 821213

The tidal approach to Cromwell Lock is straightforward and undemanding - similar to the other non-tidal locks on the Trent. Narrowboats can enter at any state of the tide. There is a floating pontoon on your starboard side, should you need to tie up. There are red and green traffic lights here as on the other Trent locks (see page 16). Once in the lock, there are vertical wires in the lock walls to pass your mooring ropes round.

Torksey Lock -
Junction with the Fossdyke & Witham Navigations.
01427 718202

Torksey Lock is in a side cut at right angles to the main river channel. A square, brick, pumping station on the riverbank at the junction is a good landmark. Do not cut the corner when entering Torksey Cut but enter mid-channel.

Once in the cut, there are floating pontoon moorings on both sides and red and green traffic lights for the lock.

Torksey Cut and moorings, viewed from the river

Torksey Lock is a manual lock operated by the lock-keeper. It is unlikely that he will be able to see you in the lock cut. Unless there is a green light showing, or you can call him on marine band radio channel 74, you will have to tie up and go in search of him (take care crossing the busy main road).
Torksey Lock can only be entered for a short time around *High Water*. Once in the lock chamber, you control your boat using your ropes around bollards on the lockside. If going up - be ready to throw your ropes up to the lock-keeper.

West Stockwith Lock – Junction with the Chesterfield Canal. 01427 890204

A party of American holiday-makers on board an Anglo Welsh hireboat wait against the lock wall whilst the lock-keeper empties West Stockwith Lock

West Stockwith lock opens directly into the tidal Trent. The bottom gates are operated electrically. They are normally kept closed because a public footpath crosses them and also to keep river silt out. They will only be opened when your arrival is imminent. The current flows swiftly past the lock entrance but there is a small patch of slack water in front of the lock and by the mooring wall to the left (Gainsborough side) of the lock.
There are no traffic lights on this lock.
The lock can only be entered for a limited time around *High Water*, usually 2½ hours before until 4 hours after.
When I arrive at this lock, I turn the boat 180degrees to face the current (when I can see down the long straight to ensure no boats are coming the other way). I then sit mid-river and give a long blast on the horn to attract the lock-keeper's attention. When the gates are open, I match the speed of the boat to the current so that we are not moving forward or back in relation to the lock. Then turn very slightly a few degrees towards the lock and feel the boat

gently drift sidewards, keeping the bow level with the lock entrance. Immediately in front of the lock entrance, there is a small amount of slack water. When your bow enters this a few feet from the lock wall, it is time to turn hard into the lock, usually requiring a strong burst on the throttle.

Many boaters entering West Stockwith for the first time turn against the flow and moor against the wall to the left-hand side of the lock. From here, the lock keeper will work you in with ropes.

Keadby Lock – Junction with the Stainforth & Keadby Canal (for the North-East Waterways). 01724 782205

Keadby lock opens directly into the River Trent. It is not easy to see where it is from a distance. Once I have passed through the former opening span of the unmistakable Keadby Bridge, I begin to cross over to the opposite side of the river - the lock is encountered after approximately half-a-mile. There are wharves either side of the lock which are occasionally occupied by barges or small coasters. As at West Stockwith, turn round against the current as you reach the lock and check if it is set ready for you. Traffic lights have recently been installed. If the lock-keeper is not visible in the new control cabin, I always give a long blast on the horn.

It is advisable to stay out in the river until summoned in by the lock-keeper. Sometimes the river in front of the wharves silts up, so at lower/later states of the tide keep in a line in front of the lock. As at West Stockwith, I match the speed of the boat to the current so that we are not moving forward or back in relation to the lock. I turn very slightly a few degrees towards the lock and feel the boat gently drift sideways, keeping the bow level with the lock entrance. When the bow is a few feet from the lock wall, I turn hard into the lock, usually requiring a strong burst on the throttle.

The chamber is wide enough to accommodate **three** narrowboats abreast.

Keadby Lock has recently been mechanised. It is unusual in that it has gates pointing in both directions so it can operate when the river levels are higher than the canal. However, tide times will usually dictate that narrowboats coming down the Trent will lock **up** into the Stainforth & Keadby Canal.

Length Restriction. Sixty feet is the normal length restriction on boats using Keadby Lock. Longer craft can only pass through when the tide in the Trent makes a level with the canal and all gates can be opened, by prior special arrangements with the lock-keeper. This means waiting outside on the tideway for appropriate conditions, and is not recommended. **Note**, that such craft will only be able to proceed as far as the similar-sized Thorne Lock.

Approaching the lock from the Stainforth & Keadby Canal, there is a road swing bridge in front of the lock which is operated by the lock-keeper. Recently installed traffic lights indicate the presence of the lock-keeper. A San.Station key will gain access through the pedestrian gate to the lock compound when the keeper is present.

Keadby Lock, viewed from the swing bridge - note the lock gates point in both directions

Contacts

Navigation Authorities
Derwent Mouth to Gainsborough - Canal & River Trust (East Midlands)
General Manager, The Kiln, Mather Road, Newark, Nottinghamshire NG24 1FB
03030 404040 (national number)
enquiries.eastmidlands@canalrivertrust.org.uk

Gainsborough to Keadby and the Humber - Associated British Ports
The Harbour Master
Associated British Ports
PO Box 1, Port House, Northern Gateway, Hull HU9 5PQ
01482-327171
www.humber.com

Locks
Cromwell Lock 01636-821213
Torksey Lock 01427-718202
West Stockwith Lock 01427-890204
Keadby Lock 01724-782205

Retford & Worksop Boat Club
Clayworth Wharf, Clayworth, Retford, Nottinghamshire DN22 9AJ
01777-817546
www.rwbc.org.uk

The Boating Association Charts
From www.theboatingassociation.co.uk, then click on the Merchandise box (half way down right-hand side of Home page). £5.00 each +p&p.
Also from the IWA, IWA Sales, Freepost NW2944
PO Box 114, Rickmansworth WD3 1WD. 01923-711114
Also, perhaps, from local boatyards and marinas.

Continued page 38

Aegre timetable.

From www.environment-agency.gov.uk, then search the site for "aegir"
A copy of the timetable can be obtained free of charge from the Environment Agency by telephoning 08708 506506. (It helps if you tell them it is in the Midlands region, and the EA uses the "Aegir" spelling).

Flood Updates

Environment Agency Floodline 0845-988-1188, then dial 1 and 052215 (non tidal) or 052225 (tidal)

Tide Tables

The most inexpensive tide table booklets are available from Fisk Printers of Hull. 01482 328677 or 222184 (ask for Hull Albert Dock only).
A more comprehensive (and therefore more expensive) booklet is available from Associated British Ports (see previous page). They are also stocked by local marinas and chandleries.
Free tidal predictions for the next six days (and predictions further ahead may be purchased) from http://easytide.ukho.gov.uk

VHF Marine Band Radio (channels p15)

All boats using VHF Marine Band Radio need to be licensed. Licensing arrangements have recently changed. Licences are now free if applied for via the internet and only need to be renewed every ten years. See www.ofcom.org.uk. Alternatively, licences can be applied for by post, but there is currently a £20 charge. Enquiries at 020 7981 3131.

Radio users require a Marine Radio Operator's Certificate of Competence. This involves taking an examination, usually included in a one-day training course. Contact the Royal Yachting Association, www.rya.org.uk, or 0845 3450377. The examinations are held at various centres around the country (Barbara and I took ours at the Waterways Museum at Goole).

Selected Marinas

Sawley Marina - 0115 973 4278
Beeston Marina - 0115 922 3168
Nottingham Castle Marina - 0115 941 2672
Farndon Marina - 01636 705 483
Torksey Diesel - 01427 718243 or 07970 936959
West Stockwith Diesel (Lock keeper) - 01427 890204

Police. Non-emergency 101

With his wife Barbara, John purchased their first boat, on the Chesterfield Canal, in 1980. They soon discovered that from that waterway they had to navigate the tidal Trent if they wanted to visit other parts of the canal system. This they have done regularly in their narrowboats over the last thirty years, subsequently covering most of the 3,000 mile canal network.

A former Chairman of the Chesterfield Canal Society, John is now Editor of that organisation's award-winning magazine *Cuckoo*. He is also an author, and a regular contributor to the national waterways press.

OTHER RICHLOW TITLES
Subsequent updates to our books on www.richlowinfo.blogspot.com

South Yorkshire Waterways Christine Richardson and John Lower. Sheffield & South Yorkshire Navigation - three canals and the Don Navigation. **(2012)** 48 pages, 14 maps.

North Yorkshire Waterways by Fiona Slee. The rivers Ouse, Ure, Foss and Derwent, plus the Ripon and Pocklington canals. **Published 2011**. 52 pages, 16 maps, 33 illustrations, spiral bound, A5 sized, colour throughout. £7.50

South Pennine Ring - Part 2 by John Lower. The Huddersfield Narrow and Broad canals, the connecting part of the Calder & Hebble. ISBN 978-0-9552609-8-8. 44 pages, spiral-bound, colour throughout, 14 maps. **Published 2011**. £7.50.

The Pennine Ring - Part 1. John Lower. **2010**. Covers the entire Rochdale and Ashton canals. Contains a wealth of information for visitors, both water and land-based. 44 pages, spiral-bound, A5 sized, colour throughout, 11 maps. ISBN 978-0-9552609-7-1. £7.50.

Chesterfield Canal - A Richlow Guide. John Lower and Christine Richardson. Through three counties - Nottinghamshire, South Yorkshire and Derbyshire - navigational information for boaters, as well as the practical points useful for other visitors - including parking and public transport, a pub and cafe listing, and easy to follow maps. Kept up to date. Spiral-bound, 44 pages, A5 sized, 12 maps, 20 coloured illustrations. £5.00.

Lincolnshire Waterways. John Lower, Christine Richardson. Updated 2009. Fossdyke, River Witham, Slea Navigation, Witham Navigable Drains, The Black Sluice Navigation, and the Horncastle Canal. Kept up to date. Spiral-bound, A5 sized, colour throughout, 60 pages, 17 maps. Navigation notes, and walking and cycling path the Water Rail Way. £7.50

Prices include post and packing. Available from www.richlow.co.uk.
books@richlow.co.uk

Stainforth & Keadby Canal (SSYN)

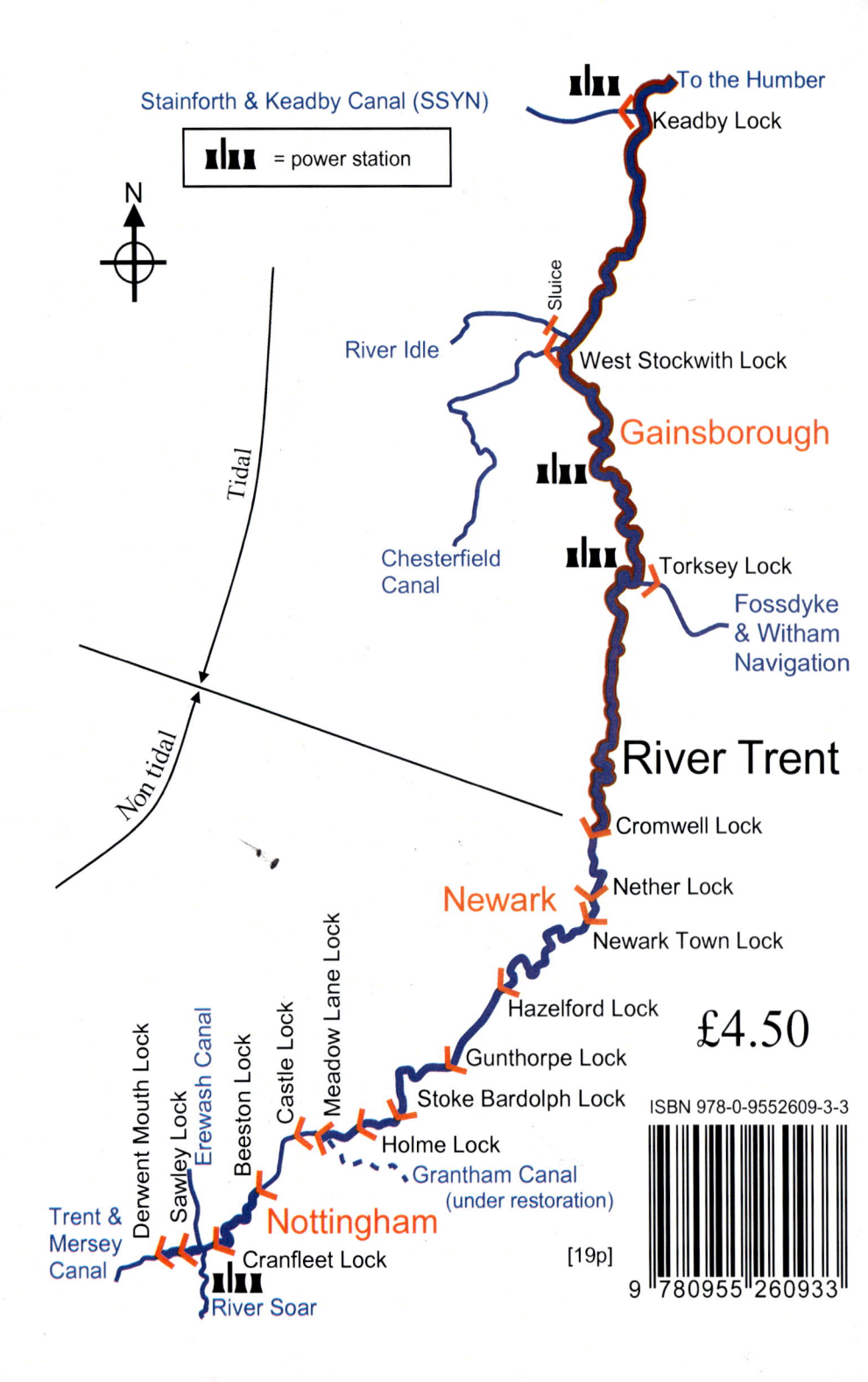

▮▮▮ = power station

N

To the Humber
Keadby Lock

Tidal

Non tidal

Sluice
River Idle
West Stockwith Lock

Gainsborough

Chesterfield Canal

Torksey Lock

Fossdyke & Witham Navigation

River Trent

Cromwell Lock
Nether Lock
Newark
Newark Town Lock
Hazelford Lock
Gunthorpe Lock
Stoke Bardolph Lock
Meadow Lane Lock
Castle Lock
Holme Lock
Beeston Lock
Erewash Canal
Grantham Canal (under restoration)
Sawley Lock
Derwent Mouth Lock
Nottingham
Trent & Mersey Canal
Cranfleet Lock
River Soar

£4.50

ISBN 978-0-9552609-3-3

[19p]

9 780955 260933